W9-BVE-140

KITTENS
AS A NEW PET

JERRY G. WALLS

CONTENTS

Photographs by Dr. Herbert R. Axelrod, Victor Baldwin, Isabelle Francais, Dorothy Holby, Linda Little, Phil Morini, Fritz Prenzel, Ron Reagan, Vincent Serbin, and Thompson Photographics.

9 8 7 6 5 4 3 2 1   **1996 Edition**   9 5 7 8 9

Distributed in the UNITED STATES to the Pet Trade by T.F.H. Publications, Inc., One T.F.H. Plaza, Neptune City, NJ 07753; distributed in the UNITED STATES to the Bookstore and Library Trade by National Book Network, Inc. 4720 Boston Way, Lanham MD 20706; in CANADA to the Pet Trade by H & L Pet Supplies Inc., 27 Kingston Crescent, Kitchener, Ontario N2B 2T6; Rolf C. Hagen Ltd., 3225 Sartelon Street, Montreal 382 Quebec; in CANADA to the Book Trade by Vanwell Publishing Ltd., 1 Northrup Crescent, St. Catharines, Ontario L2M 6P5 ; in ENGLAND by T.F.H. Publications, PO Box 15, Waterlooville PO7 6BQ; in AUSTRALIA AND THE SOUTH PACIFIC by T.F.H. (Australia), Pty. Ltd., Box 149, Brookvale 2100 N.S.W., Australia; in NEW ZEALAND by Brooklands Aquarium Ltd. 5 McGiven Drive, New Plymouth, RD1 New Zealand; in Japan by T.F.H. Publications, Japan—Jiro Tsuda, 10-12-3 Ohjidai, Sakura, Chiba 285, Japan; in SOUTH AFRICA by Lopis (Pty) Ltd., P.O. Box 39127, Booysens, 2016, Johannesburg, South Africa. Published by T.F.H. Publications, Inc.
MANUFACTURED IN THE UNITED STATES OF AMERICA
BY T.F.H. PUBLICATIONS, INC.

ACKNOWLEDGEMENTS

Persian kitten. Each and every kit has a charm all its own.

My thanks to Dr. Robert Cohen, VMD, Wrightstown, N.J., for many small courtesies over the years and to Pat Foley for a word now and then. Maleta, my wife, has always been the source of the cats in the house. Finally, to the brood that have passed through:

Calico, Apollo, Banditt, Princess, Tribbles, Checkers, Tippy, and Cricket.

INTRODUCTION

This is a book about kittens, but unavoidably it also is a book about cats. There is an obvious reason for this: kittens are just cats under about eight to twelve months in age. The healthy, happy kitten grows into a healthy, happy cat; the unhealthy, unhappy kitten ten to twelve years, often much longer. The kitten phase is short, only some five to ten percent of the entire lifetime. Also, it should be self-evident that although children may enjoy kittens, it is the parents and other adults who take care of the cat. Food bills, vet

Family of Siamese. Kittens of the same litter can be quite different in their personalities. Some are timid and shy; others are bold and outgoing. Owner, Phil Morini.

grows into a problem cat.

Normally, books on kittens are directed to children, because children are supposed to love kittens and one of the joys of childhood is growing up with a kitten. Actually, this is not quite true. Children grow up with cats, because the average cat lives some bills, vaccination schedules, and often general grooming and clean-up are the responsibilities of the adults, because children simply cannot handle the many facets of cat care. If the parents are fortunate, they will be able to have the child assume such simple tasks as litter box maintenance, casual grooming, and daily feeding, but only the time and money provided by the adults can pick a veterinarian, cope with emergencies, pay for vaccinations, and purchase the at least 2,500 cans of cat food eaten over the cat's lifetime, not to mention the toys, litter boxes and litter, treats, and the hundreds of little pieces of luggage a cat picks up during its life.

For these reasons, this book is written for the adult contemplating getting a kitten either for a child or (just as likely) for himself. After all, adults also like kittens and even the cats they grow into. I will attempt to guide you through the first year of kittenhood, from obtaining a kitten to coping with the first signs of sexuality in the cat. We'll discuss the importance of a good vet, choosing a good food from the supermarket, and just enjoying your kitten. Don't expect a lot of bull in this book about calories, protein contents, making special diets, teaching the cat to use the toilet, or cutesy names for the kitten. You can get this information elsewhere if you want it, but I don't think you need it to enjoy a kitten.

So settle back and let's start at the beginning, the birth of the kitten and its first six weeks until weaning. I know most of you will never actually see a birth or have to wean a kitten, but it is good information to have just in case . . . accidents do happen.

American Shorthair dam and kitten. If you want a kitten primarily for a pet, then you need not be concerned with its pedigree or lack thereof.

BIRTH

The birth of kittens or any other mammal (a mammal is an animal that has hair or fur, gives live birth, and suckles its young on milk; we are mammals, as are whales and seals, kangaroos, and even duckbill platypuses) is (often called a queen) have a litter is good for her and makes her more friendly and healthier in the long run, so they allow their queen to breed a least once. (Many veterinarians would strongly question the logic of this

Raising a kitten can be a rewarding experience. If you understand his ways, and how to care for him and train him, he can be a constant delight.

fascinating and a bit bloody. Since you should NEVER, NEVER, NEVER purchase or obtain a kitten until it is at least six weeks old and preferably eight weeks, you probably will never see a birth. However, many people still believe that letting a female cat argument, believing that spaying at the first heat is best and has no effect on the cat's personality.) Also, if your queen is not spayed and escapes into the world of the toms waiting outside, you certainly will have to worry about the problems of birth. Treatment of the kitten from birth to weaning at about six to eight weeks is perhaps the most important it will ever receive, so it is equally important that you understand at least the basics of what is happening to the kitten as it develops.

Of course, before you have birth, you must have sex. Cats are perhaps the most sexually inclined of familiar mammals. The mating behavior is loud, continuous, very public and (at least on the surface) a free-for-all. Basically, the queen determines the entire course of mating in the cat.

Some five thousand years ago the Egyptians or an allied people in northern Africa or perhaps the Middle East discovered that the local wild cat, *Felis sylvestris,* was very efficient at destroying the multitude of mice attacking the stored grain. They began to domesticate these wild cats and eventually (probably very quickly) produced what we call the domestic cat, an animal just one step removed from its wild ancestors and even still capable of interbreeding with it. Female wild cats came into heat or estrus, the period during which the female will accept a male for mating, perhaps twice per year. Because cats in the wild are solitary animals that seldom run across each other in the course of everyday activities, nature provided a set of behavior patterns

that allowed queens to communicate their sexual readiness to males (called "toms" today because of the name of a character in an obscure book written over two hundred years ago) over a wide area. A queen in heat starts up the most ungodly yowling and mewing you have ever had to put up with. The queen domestic cat that is kept indoors will constantly try to get outside and simply will not let up in her attempts. She also tends to release scents in both the urine and from anal and other glands to attract male cats to her; humans unfortunately cannot appreciate these exquisite scents. The Egyptians probably just let their cats out or farmed the dirty work off on the priests, but you will have to put up with this if you choose to let your cat breed.

In the old days, the owner of a queen in heat just opened the back door, let the queen out, and hoped that she went into someone else's back yard to gather her potential mates. Better to have a pregnant cat than to put up with males and females yowling continually forever. For, you see, although the wild cat ancestors of our tabbies went through heat only twice a year, domestication has changed the behavior of the domestic cat. Today, many or most queens in heat will simply stay in heat until they are bred or spayed, just going through quieter periods lasting a couple of weeks before starting the yowling again for two or three weeks at a time. When this happens, you have three choices: open the back door (certainly not a recommended solution in this age of cars, pesticides, irate neighbors, and laws about property damage and noise pollution); see your veterinarian for either spaying or a hormone shot to reduce the intensity of the heat; or breed the cat. Personally, I highly recommend spaying. If you want a litter, however, you will breed the queen.

Male cats are always ready to mate, so it isn't a great problem to find a breeder if you have a purebred cat or a friend with a willing tom whose pattern and personality you like. The queen simply is taken over to the tom, they are given a couple of days together while the queen is in heat, and you come back with a pregnant queen. This method is relatively painless and not quite so noisy as letting the queen out the

Persian kittens. Whatever breed you finally decide upon, your special kitty should be *at least* six weeks old before you bring him into your home.

back door. Its safety is assured.

If you do let the queen out, she rapidly will attract every available male in the vicinity, and all will come bearing highly scented urine and a large vocal repertoire. The queen rolls and yowls, rubs against toms, the ground, and anything else around and generally makes herself the center of attention. The toms begin a fight for dominance to be allowed to mate, with resultant scratched noses, torn ears, and ripped patches of neck hide. The winner of the fights does not necessarily get to be the first to mate with the female, however, as it seems to be strictly the queen's choice who she mates with first. It is not uncommon for a lower ranking male (especially a young tom) to stay at the edge of the fights and sneak in while the other toms are distracted. If the queen allows him to get close enough, he may become her first mate.

Mating itself is a calculated risk for the tom, as the queen is very unpredictable while excited and has a tendency to let a tom get just close enough to rip open his nose with unsheathed claws. When the tom feels that the timing is right, he sometimes not so gently attacks the female and gains a firm hold on her nape with his mouth. Because of a cat's retention of the kitten's instinct to go limp when gripped by the nape by the mother, the female relaxes a bit or at least

"If you do let the queen out, she rapidly will attract every available male in the vicinity, and all will come bearing highly scented urine and a large vocal repertoire."

does not try to rip open the tom. Using his legs and the nape grip, the tom maneuvers the queen into position for mating. She drops her head and forequarters and raises her hind quarters, also moving her tail to the side so the tom's penis can enter her vulva. Mating itself takes only a minute or two, after which the tom pulls out his penis and the queen gives vent to a blood-curdling scream. This seems to be for good cause, as the tip of the penis is covered with small but very sharp spines that actually tear the wall of the vulva when pulled out. The screaming is closely associated with ovulation, as the female releases an egg at the same time. This induced ovulation is unusual, but it assures that there is an active egg available for fertilization at the same time that sperm are present in the reproductive system. Each scream (at least the first four to six) results in an egg and probably a kitten.

This free-wheeling mating behavior may go on for an entire night or even a day, until the toms are tired of mating and the queen is sexually satisfied. By this time there will be some four to six fertilized eggs in her uterus that will develop into kittens ready for birth some sixty to sixty-three days later, sometimes a few days more, but seldom less. Because the eggs were each produced in response to a mating, it is possible for a queen

to have six kittens with six different fathers. So much for purebred alley cats.

However your queen became pregnant, you now have about two months in which to pamper her, make sure she has a balanced diet rich in proteins, fats, and calcium and other minerals, and get her used to the nesting box. If you value your clothes and furniture, be sure she gets a nesting box she likes and put it where it will be convenient for both of you. The box should be lined with clean papers (changed regularly) or towels for warmth and comfort. It should be roomy enough for the queen to stretch out in during birth but not so large that small kittens will become separated from mother. The sides should be high enough that young kittens will not be able to accidentally climb out until they are ready to face the world. Any material will do, including cardboard and plain wood, but remember that care of the nest box has to be convenient for you and the queen has to accept it.

The queen really does not need a nest box as much as you need a nest box. Queens about to give birth are notorious for their searching out of softly padded hidden places in which to give birth (sometimes called kittening, a rather strange word used in an odd fashion). Among the more normal places chosen are open drawers of clothing, the backs of closets, and corners of couches with nice cat and people scents. The middle of the bed is of course the preferred place. Since birth is a

White shorthair. Kittens experience a tremendous rate of growth during their early months of life.

rather bloody business, you definitely do not want kittens being delivered in your underwear drawer or the middle of a prize bedspread. So for your sake, provide a suitable nesting box and during the last week or two before the due date, make sure that you and the queen come to an agreement as to where to place it so it will be used.

Just before birth the queen becomes very restless, her breasts swell (breeders refer to this as the milk "dropping"), and she begins frequent trips between the nest box and the litter box. She may stop eating and drink large amounts of water. She appears to be obviously uncomfortable, and at the last minute her temperature drops about a degree. (Since a cat's temperature is taken with a rectal thermometer and even veterinarians dislike really disturbing an expectant cat, you'll probably never notice the temperature drop.) She will take to her nest box and, if a first-time mother, will actually look worried and somewhat fearful. This is the time to do what humans do best— comfort her and talk to her. Soothing talk is very helpful in making the mother-to-be relax and therefore may facilitate an easier birth.

A small splash of pinkish blood, actually the breaking of the "water sac" in the uterus, is a definite sign that birth is beginning. The female begins obvious contractions, pushing the kitten through the birth canal. In a few minutes the first kitten appears, usually head-first but often tail-first or legs-first (the latter two positions known as a breech birth, common in cats and usually no major problem). The kitten will be in a thin birth membrane or embryonic sac that the mother will immediately tear open with her teeth. She then carefully licks the kitten clean and dry and, with the stimulus of her tongue, forces the kitten to take its first breath. She will cut the umbilical cord and eat the cord and placenta (afterbirth) in an instinctive effort to reduce the signs of birth that in nature would attract predators. The afterbirth also serves as a source of hormones that may help milk production and helps prevent post-birth constipation of the queen.

The kittens often come about thirty minutes to an hour apart, but the spacing between births can be very variable, especially in an older or younger mother. If the spacing exceeds an hour or two, it perhaps is best to have a veterinarian or experienced breeder at hand. The problem with births that come less than half an hour apart is that the mother becomes very tired and does not have enough time to devote to cleaning the previous kitten. Each queen seems to set her own rate and there is little you can do about it.

Many complications can occur during birth, some minor and others life-threatening. There is little I can tell you in a book of this size, other than to be sure you know a good veterinarian or pet emergency hospital in case the worst happens. Fortunately, most queens are excellent natural mothers and major problems seldom occur. However, the number of problems seems to increase with the purity of the line—the more inbred the cat, the more likely the problems.

If for any reason the mother does not remove the kitten from the embryonic sac, you do have a problem with which you can cope. Unless you act, the kitten will suffocate in a few minutes. If the births are coming too close together for the mother to take care of the newborn, you may have to tear open the sac very gently. With a slightly moistened towel wipe off the mouth and nose and use your finger to clear any mucus or detritus from the mouth. This should clear the respiratory passages. A bit of gentle massaging of the chest or sometimes holding the kitten by the hind legs and swinging it slightly will start breathing. At other times you may have to breathe into the kitten's nose to

clear the passages and induce respiration. Kittens are delicate, but they tend to cling to life with everything they have.

The next step after the kitten is breathing with regular, even soft hoises is to cut the umbilical cord. Run your fingers gently from the kitten's belly toward the placenta, pinching the blood still in the cord away from the body. You are trying to push most of the blood out of the basal inch or so of cord that will stay attached to the kitten. Pinch the cord together about one inch from the belly and snip it with scissors. Hold the cut edges of the cord together for a few minutes to make sure there is little or no bleeding. The cut edges should adhere. Eventually the remnant of the cord will dry up and fall off. A cat has no easily recognizable belly button.

The last step is to dry and fluff

Any cat, be it a youngster or adult, should never be permitted to freely roam about outdoors.

the fur of the kitten and put it next to one of the mother's breasts. Natural instincts draw the kitten toward the nipples, and in a few minutes the three- to four-ounce, five-inch-long kitten will have slowly and blindly crawled to a favored position and attached to a nipple. The kitten seems to be able to recognize its selected nipple by scent (hard to understand for us humans with such poor noses), and each kitten in a litter will have its own preferred feeding station.

After the queen has given birth to the entire litter (sometimes just two hours, sometimes half a day), the litter should be carefully inspected to be sure all is well. Any uneaten afterbirths should be discarded and the papers or towels replaced with fresh. Remember that the queen should have unlimited access to her litter box—eating the placentas of four or more kittens can lead to a brief bout with diarrhea, which is better than the constipation that often results after birthing if the placentas are not eaten. Not all queens eat the afterbirths, however, so be aware of her litter box habits for a few days.

Other than exhaustion and occasionally a first attempt to ignore or even kill a kitten (soon overcome by natural instincts), the most serious problem in kittening is the possibility of a placenta remaining inside the uterus after

birth and serving as a source of a serious and sometimes deadly infection. Breeders usually make it a point to count afterbirths as the young appear—if you end up with, say, five kittens but only four placentas (including those eaten) accounted for, your safest bet is a quick trip to the veterinarian before anything really serious happens. He can give the queen a shot that will cause contractions and force out the trapped placenta. Anyway, it often is considered good form to have the queen and her litter looked at by your veterinarian a day or two after birthing to assess the general health of the litter and, if necessary or desired, to euthanize the kittens that are underdeveloped or simply unwanted. This may sound a bit cruel, but even the most kindhearted cat lover must recognize that there are many more cats in this world than homes for cats, and it is best to humanely put down a kitten at a very early age than to wait until it has developed a personality and then decide what to do with it.

Raising orphaned kittens under the age of four or five weeks is difficult and unlikely to succeed. If something should happen to the mother during or just after birth, you are best off consulting your vet or an experienced breeder about what to do. It is hard and time-consuming work to become a

substitute mother cat. Special substitute milks (cow's milk lacks the essential levels of proteins and fats needed by kittens) given in small doses many times a day are necessary. It also is necessary to massage the kitten's belly after meals to stimulate bowel movements. Few humans are up to such demanding work.

So now you have a litter of kittens. Assuming the mother is cooperative and dutiful in caring for the young, you can now look forward to about four weeks of relaxation.

WEEKS 1 — 6

The first six weeks or so of a kitten's life probably are the most important in its development. The kitten grows at an extremely rapid rate, learns what is expected of him as a cat, and begins to learn how he will fit into a human family. If you purchase your kitten or otherwise obtain him after he is weaned, you will never see these formative weeks, but you still should understand their importance.

At birth the kitten weighs some three to four ounces, more or less, and is perhaps five inches long from the pushed-in snout to the tip of the short tail. Although fully furred, the kitten is blind, deaf, and toothless. They are vocal animals, however, and can softly mew and even purr within a few hours of birth. Although poorly coordinated, they are able to crawl and have tiny but very sharp claws. After they have been dried by the mother and take their first breaths, one of their first actions is to actively hunt for a nipple and take their first meal, often while their mother is delivering more brothers and sisters.

For the first thirty-six to forty-eight hours the queen does not produce actual milk. Instead she produces what is called colostrum, a transparent fluid that is high in proteins and minerals and, more importantly, contains antibodies. Like other mammals, the queen is able to transmit to her offspring a partial and short-lived immunity to some of the diseases to which she has developed an immunity either naturally or through vaccination. Some scientists speculate that the colostrum also in some way helps pattern the kitten to more easily learn typical cat behaviors or even to "inherit" certain stereotyped cat behaviors. Whatever the real situation, there is no doubt that kittens allowed to feed freely on colostrum for the first day or two of their lives are healthier and less subject to illness before beginning their series of normal vaccinations. In no way does the colostrum immunity preclude the necessity of vaccinations for the major cat diseases just a few weeks later.

If the normal litter is four or five kittens, there will be plenty of milk to go around and little squabbling over choice positions. Each kitten rapidly develops a preferred suckling site and apparently can recognize its nipple

"The amount of milk available increases as the kittens grow and the demand increases, thus the mother should be given a diet rich in proteins and fats and with high levels of minerals, especially calcium."

by scent. After slowly (and soon not so slowly) crawling to a nipple, it begins to knead on the breast with its little paws, the sharp claws out. The mother does not seem to mind the claws and actually finds the kneading pleasurable. In fact, the kneading increases milk production.

The amount of milk available increases as the kittens grow and the demand increases, thus the mother should be given a diet rich in proteins and fats and with high levels of minerals, especially calcium. Vitamin supplements also would not be uncalled for now. For the first few weeks the kitten actually doubles in weight each week, so by the age of one month it should weigh about a pound and a half, depending on breed and individual body build and metabolism. This should give you some idea of just how much milk the mother has to produce to feed four or five kittens for a month.

For the first two weeks, the kittens are unable to defecate or urinate without help. This means that the mother must massage their bellies with her tongue several times a day to induce bowel movements, but since the mother seems to be continually licking and grooming her young anyway, this is not service beyond the ordinary. However, for the first two weeks she also cleans up after her kittens, eating the soft pellets

14

of feces produced and thus keeping the nest clean and without odor. Some scientists speculate (again, speculate—there is little positive evidence to back them up) that the feces of the kittens (and puppies for that matter, as mother dogs do the same thing) actually tastes sweet to the queen and she thus looks upon it as a treat. Remember that the kittens are feeding exclusively upon milk now, so the feces should be very uniform. If a kitten should appear to develop diarrhea or be constipated, see a veterinarian at once.

During the first two weeks the kittens are unable to maintain a normal adult body temperature (101.5 degrees Fahrenheit). Instead, they can hold the body at about 80 degrees Fahrenheit, depending for the rest of their warmth on the cuddling of siblings and the mother. The necessity of a warm nest box thus is obvious. From two weeks on, their body temperature becomes normal for the species.

The eyes open at about ten days, although there may be three or four days' leeway within a litter. Commonly a fine slit appears across the eye of one side, followed in a day by the other eye showing a slit. In a day or two both eyes will be fully open and the kitten's eyes will be fully visible. Occasionally defects such as blindness or genetic cataracts become visible now, but almost all cats have healthy eyes. Having the eyes open, however, does not mean that the kittens can actually see. It is likely that they really

Silver tabby American Shorthair kitten. Allowing your little feline up on the furniture is a matter of personal choice.

cannot recognize objects by sight until almost a month old. Until then they depend on scents to find their way around the nest and its immediate vicinity, although they certainly can recognize movement. The delicate whiskers also seem fully operational at an early age. Incidentally, all kittens have blue eyes, the final pigments not developing until six months or even a year after birth.

It is hard to tell just when a kitten first begins to recognize sounds as sounds, but certainly by the age of two or three weeks they will react to a bell and to footsteps.

Until about the age of three weeks, the kitten is basically immobile except for short crawls about the nest, bumping into its siblings and mother. If he has to be moved, the mother picks him up by the loose skin at the nape of the neck and carries him to the new nest location. Being lifted by the nape results in a relaxation response in which the legs dangle and the tail tucks under the body. It is not uncommon for a queen to move her litter two or three times

during this period, often for reasons that are totally obscure to humans. If she is disturbed she will move to a new spot, sometimes just a few hours after the litter is born, but just as often the move seems to us to be totally random. A mother cat can be quite single-minded about moving the nest, so perhaps it is best to let her have her way unless she is moving into a hazardous or inconvenient area.

By the age of three weeks, the

"Until about the age of three weeks, the kitten is basically immobile except for short crawls about the nest, bumping into its siblings and mother."

kitten really begins to notice that there is a world around him. He can sit up and is more in charge of his own legs and movements, trying to walk instead of crawl. With use of the legs comes more coordinated use of the paws in playing with brothers and sisters and feeling out other objects in the nest. When the kitten first is able to actively leave the nest, he becomes a "true" kitten able to play and appreciate human companionship. At this time the kitten must have access to a litter box, which he will almost immediately learn to use. Be sure the first litter box is low enough that the still wobbly kitten can enter and leave without difficulty. A shallow aluminum baking tin works well. Commonly, kittens will play and even nap in the litter box.

The teeth begin to come in at about the age of two weeks, and there should be a complete set of baby teeth (also called milk teeth) by the age of four weeks. In a complete set of milk teeth there are only incisors (the flat teeth at the front of the mouth) and canines ("eye teeth"), no molars. The baby

Siamese kittens. The age at which a cat reaches sexual maturity varies between some breeds of cat.

17

teeth gradually are replaced by the permanent teeth between the ages of fifteen and thirty weeks, with most cats having a complete set of thirty teeth more or less erupted by the age of six months. The molars develop only as part of the set of adult teeth, so the presence or absence of molars (the back teeth) and their degree of eruption are one method a veterinarian uses for determining the age of a kitten. Occasionally the incisors of the permanent dentition (set of teeth) fail to erupt completely, but almost all young cats have excellent teeth.

The three-week-old kitten has now begun to look like a real cat. He is visually alert, able to coordinate his movements to some extent, is beginning to play and interact with other kittens and objects in the nest, and is teething. In nature, this is the time at which the queen would begin to bring mice and other small animals to the nest to give the kittens their first taste of hunting. She at first would bring in completely dead prey and allow the kittens to sniff and lick it and then play with it. Later the prey is brought to the nest disabled but still alive, and eventually active prey would be allowed in the nest. In this way the kittens are taught to hunt and allowed to develop their paw-eye coordination and learn the correct killing behaviors, including the bite through the nape of the neck

that is the cat's preferred way of killing.

There is no doubt that a kitten that is not taught to hunt by his mother will still learn to mouse on his own. Even a kitten orphaned at birth will hunt and successfully kill large insects or even the occasional mouse, but there also is no doubt that his hunting technique is defective. An orphaned kitten seldom kills with a clean bite and loses more prey. Play instincts are closely related to hunting instincts, and perhaps in the domestic cat they really are not separable. All cats hunt and all cats play—some just do it better than others.

WEANING

At about twenty-one days, the queen begins to wean her kittens. This can be a simple process or a difficult one, depending on the queen and her treatment of the kittens. In nature, weaning is closely related to the teaching of hunting. As she acquaints her kittens with prey, she also begins to add regurgitated food to their milk-only menu, although at first she does not really allow them to eat prey. Her supply of milk becomes reduced as her hormones switch to a "reproductive mode" from a "kittening mode," meaning she starts becoming ready for her next mating.

The kitten now faces a difficult

and sometimes stressful situation. After three weeks of a milk diet and the warmth of the nest, he now has access to the mother less and less. As milk becomes less important in the diet, meat increases in importance and all his habits must change. Increasingly he leaves the nest to explore and play, and also to use the litter box. Mother becomes less important and the outside world more interesting.

In the home, weaning often is marked by disgruntled kittens who can't seem to understand why mother no longer allows them to feed whenever they want. At this time, the human factor in the kitten's life comes to the fore, because humans must now see him through weaning. At three weeks, the kitten is able to lick food, such as evaporated milk, from a spoon and will gladly do so because the queen no longer is producing enough milk and mice are seldom available in quantities in the average household. The weanling should take a spoonful of milk perhaps four times a day in addition to natural feedings. After a day or so, when the kitten has become fully acquainted with spoon-feeding, a readily digestible cereal food is added to the milk. Such foods are marketed as kitten foods in any supermarket or pet shop, with a great number of brand names available. It is always best

to purchase well-known brands of food and, in my opinion, you should not try to save a few pennies by purchasing an off-brand or no-brand product. A good kitten food digests readily and has vitamin and mineral supplements. In theory, it will provide a complete and balanced diet for the growing kitten.

The kitten will rapidly learn to accept the milk and cereal mixture and will look forward to its feedings about four or five times a day, with occasional between-meal snacks. By the third or fourth day you should be able to teach him to feed from a shallow bowl by either gently holding his head on the edge of the bowl until he realizes it

Abyssinian adults and litter of kittens. Establishing a successful cat breeding program demands a considerable amount of time, money, and energy.

contains food or (perhaps more certain and less traumatic) the spoon can be maneuvered to the edge of the dish while the kitten is feeding, in the hope that he will just continue feeding on the food in the dish. Kittens are fast learners, especially where food is concerned.

Although kitten foods are supposed to be complete diets, most owners supplement this food with meat. Somehow this seems more natural than feeding only cereal, as in nature the kitten would be eating regurgitated and partially digested prey by four weeks of age and even making his own attempts at hunting and killing prey. Finely diced lean muscle meat (not liver, which may cause diarrhea in some kittens) can be added to the porridge by the end of week four and will be accepted readily by the weanling. In saying lean meat, I follow what almost all the books say, but I personally have my doubts about leaving fat out of the diet of kittens. Cats require more fat in the diet than do dogs, and this must also apply to kittens. Certainly mother's milk is rich in fats and the expression "a nice fat mouse" as used in so many cat and mouse cartoons has a basis in fact. Kittens often have a strong preference for bologna and other high-fat processed meats, including such things as chicken frankfurters and even a bit of liverwurst. Be careful of diarrhea when feeding the kitten his first meat meals. It might be best in the case of longhairs to trim the hair near the anus close to the skin to make grooming easier and accidents less common.

By the end of the kitten's fourth week of life, he should be active, constantly exploring and playing when not sleeping. He should be using a litter box regularly with few or no accidents. He should be attempting to groom himself regularly. He should be eating a mixture of milk, cereal, and perhaps meat about four times a day. Most importantly, he should be less dependent on mother than on humans now. For at the beginning of his fifth week he is officially on his own and ready to become your pet for the next ten or fifteen years.

CHOICES

If you are purchasing a kitten or adopting one, your contact with a kitten will begin after the kitten is a month old. Under no circumstances should you even consider purchasing a kitten that is time it is stressed. Obviously, leaving the sanctuary of the nest with mother and brothers and sisters is highly stressful, especially since the kitten now has to adapt to human companionship

Burmese kitten. Members of this breed are active, friendly felines who will enjoy your company, but are less demanding than some other breeds of cat, such as the Siamese.

under five weeks of age and preferably six weeks old. Many breeders will not allow a kitten to leave its siblings until almost two months of age. The reason is very simple: until the kitten is fully weaned and adjusted to a regular kitten diet it is in danger every and the various things a human expects of him. His diet is different, strange toys and objects such as furniture appear in his life, and great human bodies and faces, as well as feet, constantly intrude into everything he does.

Now, where can you get a

kitten? The answer is fairly obvious: almost anywhere. If you look in the classified ads of your local newspaper you will see kittens being offered free to a good home. If you drive down almost any country road you will find a sign offering free kittens. Any pet shop in a mall will have kittens for sale. You probably know someone at work or school who is trying to give away a kitten. The problem is to decide just what you want in a kitten and what is the best kitten for you.

First, the sex of the kitten. Cats are fairly discrete when it comes to showing their sex, and kittens are often very difficult to sex. Lift the kitten up by the tail so the hind legs just leave the floor. This gives a clear view of the anus and surrounding areas. Below the anus will be another opening, the opening of the urethra, through which the kitten urinates. Unlike puppies, in which males have a distinct sheath about the urethral opening, kittens just have a simple papilla and opening. The important point in sexing is the distance between the anus and the urethra. In males the testes will eventually (by six months or so) extend from the body in a sac or scrotum that will occupy the space between the two openings. In females this area stays simple. For this reason there is a longer space between the anus and urethra in male kittens than in

females, a difference best understood by examining several kittens of both sexes. With a little bit of practice, the distinction is clear—a wide space is a male, a small space is a female. However, even breeders commonly make mistakes in sexing kittens, especially young kittens, so don't feel bad if your little girl later turns out to be your little boy. It happens all the time with cats. Either way, you should have the cat neutered at the proper time to prevent all types of problems. More on this later.

Does the sex of the kitten really make a difference in the quality of the pet? I doubt it. Until they become sexually mature, kittens are all fairly alike in personality. No two kittens are exactly alike, but they all fall within rather narrow limits of personality. Some are shyer than others, some bolder. Some are extremely active, others only very active (a truly lazy kitten probably is a sick kitten). If you treat your kitten well and adjust him or her to life with a human family, it will turn into a nice cat. This of course assumes that males are neutered and females spayed at the proper time. If cost is a consideration, then select a male, because the cost of the neutering operation is probably going to be about a third of the cost of spaying a female.If you plan on (horrors!!) letting your cat run loose, get a

"If you treat your kitten well and adjust him or her to life with a human family, it will turn into a nice cat."

male—at least he won't return home pregnant. Many people feel that females are more affectionate than males, but this is not true once the cat has been neutered. A well-adjusted kitten will grow into an affectionate cat, regardless of sex.

Longhair or shorthair? All cats shed, so the length of their hair probably is irrelevant in this regard. Personal taste and how much time you have available for grooming should determine your choice. A longhaired cat has to be combed regularly, especially when young, or it will turn into a mess of mats. Matted kittens are unsightly, often irritable (mats hurt), and costly to bring to a groomer for hair repair. Many people find that combing and brushing a kitten is a very relaxing way to spend a few minutes each day, while others find it a chore. Children probably cannot be depended upon to groom a longhaired cat regularly and properly, so it will become the responsibility of the parent. Shorthaired cats have to be groomed also but are more forgiving about going a week or two with nothing but a casual combing. Even shorthairs mat in the armpits and under the throat, however, so don't expect to never have to comb and brush a shorthair. No one clips a cat like they clip dogs, so you are stuck

with your decision. Think carefully about your lifestyle before deciding on coat length.

How about a calico? A calico is a tricolored female (white with black and red patches), the result of a very specific type of inheritance. Calicos are never males because the calico gene is what is known as lethal, meaning that any male kittens carrying the calico gene die before birth. In personality and behavior, calicos are perfectly normal cats, but at least you are certain of their sex. They also are very attractive, and many people prefer them to other color patterns. Calicos occur as both longhairs and shorthairs. My wife has always been partial to calicos because her first cat was a calico, and it would be difficult to imagine not having one around the house.

So where should your kitten come from? Probably the best answer is "anywhere you can find a healthy kitten." I stress the "healthy" because this will follow your kitten throughout its life. The problem with free kittens is that you often know very little about them and their pre-weaning weeks. Also, because it is free, an owner might have a tendency to not value the kitten as highly as should be. If you pay for something, you think twice before doing anything that might be detrimental to it, even something as simple as not regularly grooming it.

For these reasons I recommend purchasing a kitten from a reputable pet shop or from a breeder (especially if you are interested in a purebred). Pet shops have advantages and disadvantages. The main advantage is ease of selections. Almost any pet shop will have a half dozen kittens, in various colors and hair lengths, and usually of about the same age. There may be a few near-purebreds available. Cost usually is reasonable for a regular kitten, probably about the same as you will spend on the odds and ends you need to purchase to keep it plus the basic veterinarian visit. The pet shop also sells all the items you will need to have when you take the kitten home.

These advantages are to some extent balanced by the fact that you can never be sure of the age and ancestry of a pet shop kitten. Some dealers purchase from large-scale breeders of doubtful ethics who may sell kittens as young as three weeks and seldom more than four weeks old. Such young kittens often cannot take the stress of a new home as they are barely weaned. A reputable pet shop will be able to assure you that the kitten is at least five weeks old, and this will be corroborated by your veterinarian.

In several states there are consumer laws that place limits on a pet shop sale. Such laws usually require that any kitten must have a veterinarian's certificate of health obtained within one or two weeks of the purchase. If the veterinarian discovers serious health faults in the kitten, the pet shop must accept a return of the kitten and refund any purchase price (sometimes including the cost of the vetting) or provide a satisfactory replacement. These laws protect both the consumer and the shop. Kittens of the proper age usually are healthy, but occasionally poor specimens do make it to the shop. Virtually all kittens have worms, for instance, a condition that is treated by the vet on your first visit. In some kittens the infestation may be so heavy that health is threatened. Occasionally there will be genetic defects such as cataracts or fused vertebrae that may not be obvious except to a veterinarian. No pet shop wants to gain a reputation for knowingly selling unhealthy animals, but such things do happen.

Breeders are the best place to purchase purebred kittens. By definition a purebred is a cat that has papers saying it is a purebred. Because there are many cat registry organizations (as opposed to just a few in any country registering dogs), the standards of a purebred will vary considerably, but usually within obvious limits. A breeder can explain to you just why their line of kittens is registered with a particular organization and how one breed differs from another. In truth, the basic breeds of cat are all very similar (except for the few breeds that have actual physical differences such as the Manx) in personality. Choice of breed is dependent on personal taste, simple likes and dislikes. If you like Siamese and don't care for Persians, that is your decision. Just remember that you will have to live with your choice for at least ten years.

Breeders can be found in the directory pages of cat magazines or by contacting the various registry organizations for lists of local breeders (again, see the various newsstand cat magazines). Often a pet shop will be able to special-order a purebred for you, but this really does not allow you to see a bunch of kittens and make a real decision. Just because a kitten is a purebred does not mean

he is healthy or has an exceptional personality. It should mean, however, that you can inspect the conditions under which he grew up and get to know his mother and siblings. Because you are dealing directly with a breeder, you also can be sure of the age of the kitten, because breeders keep litter records on dates of mating and birth. As with the pet shop kitten, be sure to take your purchase to a veterinarian within a few days of taking it home and have it vetted. In some states breeders are subject to the same laws as pet shops concerning the health of a kitten.

A purebred kitten will cost you several times that of a pet shop kitten but you will have registration papers with it that will allow you to show the cat in cat shows if you wish and will let you register offspring if certain rules of mating are followed. If you have a purebred you probably will not

A "rainbow" litter of Abyssinian kittens: red, blue, ruddy, and fawn. No matter what its breed, the kitten you choose should be alert and interested in its surroundings.

25

want to have it neutered, which of course will lead to problems when the female comes into heat or the male starts spraying. Personally, I like common house cats as long as they are healthy and have a good personality. Lineage means little for a pet other than expense. Additionally, I believe that at least some lines of purebreds are in some way weaker than "average" cats and more subject to illnesses. If you feel differently, and many people would certainly not agree with me, then feel free to buy a purebred.

I mentioned that you should have several kittens to choose from. There is a very good reason for this: kittens often make the choice for you. Some kittens are naturally attracted to certain people and are not afraid to show their attraction. If the kitten is healthy and has the other requirements you want, personality should be your tie-breaker in making the decision.

A healthy kitten will be active, playing with toys and any other kittens. It should react when you pick it up, hopefully by just arching the back and hissing, although some kittens swat. The incisors and canine teeth should be developed, the eyes clear and not watery, and the anus free of dried feces adhering to the hairs (indicating diarrhea). By the time you should be seeing a kitten it

should be litter-box trained (except for the little accidents all babies have). It also should be fully weaned and accepting a normal kitten food without additional milk. This is very important, because as I have repeatedly stated, unweaned kittens react poorly to stress and will cause problems that you do not want. In other words, the kitten should be ready to go home with the least bit of bother.

The following is an unpaid editorial. Never purchase a kitten that is declawed or ever seriously consider having the operation done. I know that kittens and cats occasionally are scratchers and it is hard to either train them to leave the furniture alone or protect favored spots from their attention. You should be able to train a kitten to leave furniture alone, and even adults can be "encouraged" to scratch somewhere else. Declawing is an inhumane operation that changes the essential nature of the cat. Without its claws a cat is defenseless. It cannot mouse successfully and even has trouble with certain types of play. If you cannot cope with a cat's claws, then find a new home for the cat. Additionally, declawing sometimes does not work and the claws will grow back. In my opinion there is nothing to recommend declawing under any circumstances.

"Declawing is an inhumane operation that changes the essential nature of the cat. Without its claws a cat is defenseless."

26

Tabby shorthaired kittens. A cat of undetermined lineage can make a wonderful and hardy pet and is just as easy to love as the most expensive pedigreed kitten you can buy.

A third source of kittens should be mentioned: the local humane society. In some areas, well-organized and helpful animal welfare societies aid in placing unwanted cats with good homes. For little more than the cost of the basic vaccinations and agreeing to a neutering contract, the kitten of your choice is yours. I personally have a problem with this type of adoption, but must admit that it works well in some areas. There certainly are more kittens than homes for kittens, and I guess I should welcome anything that reduces the number of unwanted kittens. Two basic problems arise, however.

The first is that some animal welfare shelters are unreliable. They are under-financed and run by people with more good intentions than resources. Such shelters may skimp on the proper food and hygiene as well as proper veterinary care. Because they

come and go they cannot even attempt to enforce neutering contracts.

The second problem is that in some cases adoptions are too casual, the shelter just trying to move out another mouth to make room for another unwanted kitten. Because the kittens were unwanted to begin with, there is no guarantee that they had a healthy first month of life and they may present problems later. If you do consider using an adoption service of any type, it would be best to discuss it with your veterinarian before getting the kitten. For that matter, it is always best to find a reliable veterinarian before you obtain a kitten—better safe than sorry.

PUREBREDS

For some reason that is inexplicable to me, some people insist on having only purebred kittens. I will be the first to admit that I have never owned a purebred, and I am not ashamed of this fact. Our cats have always been "normal" cats, simple sturdy animals with unclassifiable color patterns and very uncertain heritage. I have never seen a "normal" cat with a really bad personality, nor one that would not respond to attention and affection. Everything I have read about purebreds and gained through conversation with people with purebreds makes me think that many (but not all) are physically weaker than ordinary cats and more subject to bad reactions to even minor stresses. Other than the purebreds that closely resemble ordinary cats in shape (such as American Shorthair, Abyssinian, Oriental Shorthair, and Maine Coon Cat), I personally find some breeds to be an affront to the ancestry and dignity of the cats that came before.

Obviously this is a minority opinion, as many people like purebreds and pay significant sums to obtain them. As I see it, one of the major problems of purebred cats is that, as compared to purebred dogs, all cats basically are the same. The differences between all but the most extreme breeds are very minor, such as length of coat and exact color of fur and eyes. Dogs have been bred for specific purposes for literally centuries, so there are well over one hundred obviously different breeds plus numerous less distinct ones. Cats have always been cats until relatively recently, and there simply are few really obvious differences.

Because of this lack of distinctions, a purebred is defined (at least by me) as a cat that someone has declared to be a purebred. Admittedly there are registry organizations (one major and several minor just in the United States) that keep track of breeding records through forms known as pedigrees and write what are known as standards for a breed (what the breed is supposed to look like), but they seldom agree among themselves as to the characters that define a breed. When you cross international boundaries, the problems are even larger, and only a "cat lawyer" could really understand why an American Tonkinese is not at all like a British Tonkinese.

Considering my attitude about purebreds, you obviously cannot expect me to write glowingly about the various available breeds. I suggest that before you consider purchasing a pedigreed cat you do some research on your own. Talk to several breeders and visit at least two who breed the type of cat you like. Read a book or two (a good start would be scanning Kelsey-Wood's *Atlas of Cats of the World*, T.F.H. Publications) and purchase one or more of the

28

A lovely Korat. Length of coat, whether short or long, is one important criterion in selecting your feline: longcoated breeds will require a more extensive grooming regimen than shortcoated breeds.

newsstand cat magazines. You will be paying a rather large sum of money for a good purebred cat, so the investment in time and reading material will be worth your while.

Once you have decided just which breed you desire, the usual requirements for kitten health and early history apply. Kittens are all very much alike, and certainly you will not want to endanger your "investment" (yes, some people look at purebreds as an investment or at least a status symbol) by failing to give it the proper care and veterinary attention.

Purebreds are in many ways ranked by their pedigrees. This is a detailed record of the matings that over several generations led to your kitten. Here you will find the names of the parents, grandparents, etc., which allows an expert to evaluate the background of the kitten. Purebreds are registered with an organization that, within limits, provides a type of guarantee that the kitten really belongs to its breed and has a certain and defined ancestry. Possession of the registry certificate will allow you to show your cat in shows for points toward championships and also allow you entry to the rather mystical world of breeding of purebreds. If you do not have a registry certificate you probably do not really have a purebred kitten.

Unlike "normal" cats, neutering is not recommended for registered purebreds. There are obvious monetary reasons for this that make it reasonable to put up with the trials and tribulations of cat sex. The potential for mating your kitten when it matures should be discussed with the breeder when you make your purchase (actually, it might be considered one of the things to talk about long before you make the purchase because it is so important). You sometimes may be able to obtain a kitten that for various not very obvious reasons does not quite measure up to the standards of a breeder or does not fit into the breeder's plans for developing the line. Such kittens may be available rather cheaply if they come with a contract that says you must neuter the animal and not allow it to breed. Such kittens may still be registered and definitely are purebreds, but they just don't come up to the exacting standards of the breed. You probably will never be able to see why the kitten doesn't quite make it, and it will make just as good a pet as a breedable purebred.

Cat shows are complex ranking competitions with abundant rules that must be covered in other books (*Show Your Cat* by Meins and Floyd, T.F.H. Publications, is fairly basic and understandable). Few purebreds are good show animals, because it takes more than just matching breed standards

to gain points in competition. Show cats need a certain type of personality that lets them put up with the rigors of a show career and the constant grooming and poking essential for showing. Frankly, few self-respecting ordinary cats would put up with what a show cat must take every week—baths, grooming, clipping, coat additives, being confined in small quarters for hours at a time, and constantly traveling from one show to another. In fact, few people are cut out to put up with the rigors of a show career.

Over three dozen breeds are recognized by American registry organizations, with about the same number—with several differences—recognized by the British. Over three-quarters of the cats registered by the largest American registry, the Cat Fanciers' Association (CFA), are Persians, longhairs so familiar to any cat person. Another six percent or so are Siamese. The other breeds therefore are relatively rare even though some look very familiar and get a lot of press, such as Abyssinians and Manx. Himalayans are basically Persians with color at the points (the ears, muzzle, feet, etc.), a genetic feature that pops up in other breeds as well. Several breeds, such as the Exotic Shorthair, Bombay, and Havana Brown, are the result of purposeful crosses of major older breeds followed by selective breeding to get a somewhat different-appearing purebred line. Some breeds are the result of mutations, random natural changes in the genes that produce a recognizable difference that can be inherited. Typical examples of mutational breeds are the Manx (with fused

and largely unknown outside the cat world.

The world of purebreds is in many ways different from the world of ordinary cats, at least beyond the basic similarities of care. If you decide on a purebred, do not make the decision without considerable thought and planning. Only breeders can really tell you

Cornish Rex. This unusual breed of cat is named for both the rex mutation that produces a wavy coat and the Cornwall region of Great Britain, where a cat of this type first appeared in 1950.

and otherwise defective vertebrae that produce a tailless condition and a hopping gait), Sphynx (a hairless or nearly hairless little monster that is a cat only by definition), Scottish Fold (a minor mutation that produces a folded ear in an otherwise normal cat), and Rex (with short, tightly curled fur). The mutational breeds have their followers, but because they appear so bizarre and often are difficult to breed, they remain rare

what their breed is like, its good and bad points. After you purchase the kitten, you will need to stay in contact with a breeder to get the most out of the breed in terms of showing and mating. To many people this is what cats are all about, the thrill of shows and the chase of the perfect pedigree. If this appeals to you, go for it. As for me, I'll take a plain old tabby intent on scratching the corner of the couch.

ACCESSORIES

Now that you have selected your kitten and are ready to take it home, you need to have a few items for his and your convenience. All these items are relatively cheap and readily available from your local pet shop.

First, you will need a litter box. Until the kitten is about two or

a small litter box. Cats like roomy boxes and will soon outgrow the small sizes. If you provide your kitten with the shallow pan and also give it a full-size box with litter, you will be astounded how rapidly he will learn to use the larger box.

Our cats use a covered box,

three months old he will not be able to use a regular cat box because getting in and out will be too difficult. For the first couple of months you can use aluminum baking pans (the disposable kind is fine and cheap), starting relatively small and low and getting larger and higher as the kitten grows. The litter box should be at least as long as the kitten's body plus tail. My suggestion is to purchase a couple of cheap baking pans and, the same day you purchase the kitten, buy the litter box he will use as an adult. Never waste money buying

which I find to be very convenient and hygienic. Not all cats, supposedly, will use covered boxes, though I have no reason to believe this. Some cats (and remember, your little kitten will soon be a cat) have a tendency to "aim high" when urinating, and a cover helps prevent messes. Put a couple of layers of paper under the box just in case.

I've never used the plastic box liners that seem to be very popular now, but I've no reason to doubt that they are handy and probably cut down a bit on the mess of use a scratching post from day one, you may avoid the trials of damaged furniture later. Cricket, one of our current brood, never was actually taught to use a post, and today we pay for this with a slightly torn couch corner. At the moment, she has decided that a new chair seat is excellent scratching material, which will lead to lots of yelling and probably a few exchanges of flat of the hand and paws. Teach the kitten early or regret it later.

Scratching posts come in many styles and probably will be the most expensive item you will have to purchase for the kitten. The cheapest is actually a pad of corrugated cardboard with the corrugated edges up, the whole thing held together by a cardboard case. Kittens rapidly learn to jump on this and stretch out to work the claws. The more typical post is actually an upright cylinder covered with loosely woven fabric of some type. There commonly is a bell or other toy on top attached to a spring to make it twist wildly. Kittens learn to climb such a post to get to the toy. Although excellent, these are rather expensive and tend to have bases that are too weak to take the weight and momentum of a kitten, let alone an adult cat. A good compromise is a fabric-covered pad that hangs from a convenient and sturdy doorknob. Other scratching posts are basically limbs or sections of tree trunk with the bark intact. These seem quite adequate for most cats, although I've personally never had one.

You don't need to purchase bowls for food and water, but it helps. Any metal or ceramic bowls of the appropriate size will do as long as the metal is not soluble (certainly nothing with teflon or copper bottoms) and the ceramics are safe for human use (no lead or heavy metals in the glaze). The water bowl should have a wide bottom and be relatively heavy to prevent tipping. My personal experience is that you should never use plastic for water and food bowls. Even supposedly safe plastics eventually leach out chemicals to which cats may be sensitive. Checkers, one of our eighteen-year-olds, once came down with a horrible case of "cat acne," a polite name for sores and

Your pet shop carries a variety of litter boxes from which you can choose. Whichever style you decide upon, make sure it is roomy enough to comfortably accommodate your pet. (Pictured is a Himalayan owned by Marianne Lawrence.)

changing litter. They are moderately expensive and probably not really necessary. Try some and see how they work for you.

You also will need a litter scoop. Don't convince yourself that some kitchen utensil can be converted into a scoop. Actually, scoops probably are cheaper than kitchen utensils. I find that the plastic scoops you normally see often are poorly made and break under normal usage within a couple of months. Try to find a metal scoop with slightly upturned edges. This design may be hard to find but you will appreciate the effort later.

Next is the litter. There must be a dozen different brands of litter available in any store you check. All probably work, but all are not equal. There are pelleted alfalfa litters, modified corn cob litters, treated paper litters, and scented and unscented clay litters. Unless you want to experiment, my suggestion is to purchase a name-brand litter of white clay that is weakly or not scented. I have never noticed any difference between scented and unscented litters and cats sometimes do not like scented litters. I do notice a very important difference in litter colors, however. Dark clay litters that turn almost black when wet are very difficult to clean as the feces disappear into the wet litter.

Litters that only darken a bit when wet make feces more obvious. This may sound like an inane point, but after you have dug around in a cat box for a few years you will appreciate the difference. None of our cats has ever liked the alfalfa litters, and at least one refused to use it. I've never tried the corn cob or treated paper litters. Don't waste your time trying sand or crumpled newspaper—you've never seen such as mess as trying to clean urine-soaked footprints off the furniture. Litter is relatively cheap and you'll find you can't live without it.

With a single cat you probably should change the litter at least once a week, depending on the cat's metabolism. Some kittens are dainty, others messy. Before putting new litter in the box it sometimes helps to spray the box with an odor absorber. Use at least an inch of litter, perhaps two. Any deeper and the cat will just have fun digging and tossing it out of the box.

The next item of self-protection you will need is a scratching post or pad. Cats, including kittens, are constantly scratching in loose fabric to remove the old claw sheaths to let the sharp new claws come to the surface. If you look at a scratching post you often will see old claw sheaths buried in the fabric. If you teach the kitten to

"Litter is relatively cheap and you'll find you can't live without it."

33

blisters on the lower jaw. Normally this is caused by poor grooming, but in this case nothing seemed to help. The usual antibiotics caused the sores to disappear for a few days or weeks, then they returned. Out of desperation we removed the usual plastic water and food dishes and replaced them with ceramic and stainless steel. In a week the sores disappeared and never returned. Not a very scientific experiment, but enough to make me stay away from plastics. A paper or plastic mat under the dishes helps make messes smaller and easier to clean up; some kittens are very messy eaters.

The last essential items are toys. Kittens need to play and will make their own toys if necessary, but purchased toys probably are safer in the long run. For young kittens, avoid toys with small bells, button eyes, and other parts that might be swallowed. Unless you are there to supervise, don't offer ribbons or string to a kitten. Some kittens start chewing on a ribbon and then seem unable to stop. This can lead to severe impaction of the gut and a trip to the veterinarian. In really bad cases an operation may be necessary. Play safe and give the kitten a ribbon only if you are there to pull it. Many years ago Banditt managed to steal some Christmas present wrappings and ate at least three feet of ribbon. A

trip to the vet resulted, and fortunately there was no serious damage. However, for the next week every visit by Banditt to the litter box ended with a frenzied run around the house, feces and length of ribbon dragging behind. After you've had to cut feces and ribbon off your kitten for a week you will learn to be careful with string and ribbons.

Kittens love to chase things, so

Scratching posts offer hours of healthy exercise and enjoyment for cats and kittens while preventing them from damaging the furniture. Photo courtesy of Cosmic Pet Products.

balls of appropriate size and texture (always soft, never hard) are excellent. The usual catnip-stuffed mice and so on also are good for batting around, but don't expect your kitten to get excited over catnip. Catnip exerts an influence only over sexually mature cats, and then not over every cat. Catnip does not harm, however. Rattling toys hanging from a string (securely tied) are also greatly appreciated. A paper bag always excites a cat, who can spend literally hours examining its mysteries. The same goes for a ball of paper and a feather.

You also will need grooming tools and a few essential health products, but we'll talk about these later.

Now that you have everything, you can take the kitten home. Oh yes, almost forgot. Just how do you get him home? Kittens don't fit too well in shopping bags. Do yourself a favor and buy a good cat carrier. Many different styles are available, from very cheap ones that look like cardboard boxes (and work about as well) to good plastic and metal ones used to ship pets on airlines. You will need the carrier when you take the kitten to the vet and any time you put him in the car. (Don't think you can hold a kitten or cat while driving—my wife tried it once and ended up blowing out two tires on a curb.) If you purchase a carrier, buy one large enough for an adult cat, not a kitten. They are expensive items and kittens soon grow up and will need a larger carrier. If you put a cushion in the carrier and leave the door open it will serve well as the kitten's bed and private corner to get away from things. Every kitten needs a private place.

Catnip, which has long been a feline favorite, will provide your pet with hours of enjoyment. Photo courtesy of Cosmic Pet Products.

FEEDING

Feeding a kitten today is a relatively simple process. There is no need to prepare special mixtures unless you want to and no need to stock up on exotic and smelly "waste meats." Today many stores, including your local pet shop, sell a broad variety of not even need saying. From the age of at least three weeks a kitten needs access to a bowl of clean water on demand. Some cats are heavy drinkers, others light, but all need water twenty-four hours a day.

Your kitten's first food at home

Persian kittens. A well-fed kit will have boundless energy and a zest for exploring its environment.

healthy packaged foods suitable for the kitten and the cat he grows into. For our purposes foods fall into four categories: canned meat foods; moist envelope foods; dry foods; and supplements and treats. Water also is an essential in the kitten's diet, which would seem to (assuming of course that he is fully weaned) will be a dry cereal-based food, actual kitten food. There are many types, but all the name-brand products provide good nutrition. They contain a cereal plus vitamins and minerals, usually with powdered milk and

37

some meat meals. At first the kitten food should be mixed with water to soften it and give it a more milk-like consistency, but in a few weeks the kitten will eat it dry. Generally, follow feeding instructions on the package. A simple rule is to feed a kitten all it will eat at least four times a day. It doesn't hurt to have dry food (changed each day) in a small bowl for between meal snacks. As long as plenty of water is available separately, a kitten over eight weeks old should have no problems.

It doesn't hurt to supplement the dry food or food/water mix with small pieces of meat. As mentioned earlier, many kittens really go crazy over chicken franks or bologna. Moderation is the name of the game on all such extras, however.

Canned foods are based on meat or fish and contain a high amount of moisture proportionate to total weight of the can. They thus are not as economical as dry foods, but cats love them and many people prefer to feed them. The usual can is about six or six and a half ounces in weight, although recently single-serving cans of three ounces or less have appeared on the market. For a single cat or a kitten, the small cans probably are best as many cats don't like refrigerated leftovers. A kitten commonly will eat two or three ounces of canned food per meal—less if dry food is also available.

Not all canned foods are equal. The large cans (ten ounces and more) often contain a great amount of corn meal and other fillers that simply are not acceptable to kittens or cats. Read the labels and stay away from cheap foods with lots of meal. If meat or fish is not listed first or second in the list of ingredients, your cat probably will not like the food.

This brings up the question of fish. Many books were written in an age when kitten owners cooked up fish for their pets because it was cheap and kittens went crazy for it. Two problems exist with fish. First, fish contains an enzyme that neutralizes certain vitamins, at least if not cooked. Second, fish oils in high concentrations could lead to some serious dietary complications. Today's fish-based canned foods are relatively safe as the fish is fully cooked and vitamins are added just in case. Kittens still go crazy over fish, however, which is a problem in itself. It is all too easy to give in to a kitten's choices of food, giving him just the flavors he likes. If this happens you will soon be trained to obey your pet's every whim, since giving the "wrong" flavor results in crying, not eating, and looks of disgust. After a couple of days the kitten probably also will begin to cry and look at you with

"Not all canned foods are equal...Read the labels and stay away from cheap foods with lots of meal. If meat or fish is not listed first or second in the list of ingredients, your cat probably will not like the food."

38

disgust. Kittens and cats all too readily get hooked on favorite foods. Don't let this happen. Feed a wide variety of flavors and try to be sure that fish flavors form less than half the canned food.

In the past few years, moist pellets in foil envelopes or cans have become quite popular. Many cats love the stuff, and I guess it is as healthy as anything else. It is expensive, however, and the waste ratio is high. After being exposed to air for ten or twelve hours, the moist pellets turn to rocks and no cat will look at them twice.

The routine we follow is very simple and consists of giving all of the three foods discussed above. As a basic meal the cat gets canned food. Bowls containing dry food and moist food are available all day. A kitten will do well on such a diet, as there will always be food available to fill his voracious appetite and there should be plenty of vitamins and minerals available.

As mentioned, a young kitten should be fed at least four times a day as much as he will eat. When the permanent teeth begin to come in at about four to five months the appetite probably will decrease a bit because of the pain of teething. By this time the kitten will be taking three meals a day. With the onset of sexual maturity and full growth (by about one year), the cat can go down to just two meals a day. This assumes that dry food

and water are available on demand all day.

All cats have built-in watches and alarm clocks. Within a week your kitten will expect to be fed at certain times and will get very upset if the food isn't there. Set up a feeding schedule with regular hours and stick to it.

The diet of male cats has an additional wrinkle, that of possible urinary blockage. For some reason a semisolid mucus clogs the urethra, making urination impossible. If not detected immediately through observation of unusual straining in the litter box, the cat could die. Some workers believe this condition is due to excess ash (insoluble residue) in the food, but others doubt this. Discuss the problem with your veterinarian early in the kitten's life and follow his

If you have more than one kitten, it is fine to let them share a food bowl, as long as each kit gets his fair share. Some kittens are more aggressive than others and may bully their siblings at meal time.

opinion. Most better grade cat foods, canned and dry, list the ash percentage on the label.

One final word about dry foods—eating dry food helps clean the teeth through simple physical abrasion and perhaps helps prevent tartar build-up at the base of the teeth. This could lead to fewer dental problems as the cat grows older.

Although not technically foods, vitamin and mineral supplements are available for kittens and cats. Today's commercial foods are well-balanced, so there probably is no need for the routine giving of supplements, although they are good if the kitten is ill and during any times of stress. During its first few months, mineral supplements may actually help the rapidly growing kitten achieve full size with sturdy bone structure.

One type of supplement that is handy to have around is the high-calorie liver-flavored type that comes in a tube. Available under various names, these supplements are excellent as foods during emergencies, as when the kitten suddenly becomes sick and won't take ordinary foods. It also is handy to refresh an over-active kitten that has been too active for his own good and simply used up all its available blood sugar. It provides a spurt of energy and can even be used as an only food in special cases. No pet home should

be without it.

Although the problem may never arise, occasionally the kitten or cat owner has to make a decision about letting a kitten eat a wild animal it has caught. Kittens are notorious fly-catchers and moth-eaters. These probably do no harm. If an occasional mouse is caught it probably will be played with and killed, but seldom will a pet cat kept indoors actually eat a mouse. Perhaps this is just as well because of the worms and other parasites a mouse carries. If a kitten should happen to catch a bird or find one recently dead, however, it will eat it or try to eat it. Few cats can catch a healthy bird, so it is likely that any bird the kitten ends up with was sick or even dead when found. It is not a good idea to let the kitten eat a bird. Without making too much of a fuss, gently take it away from him and replace it with a treat or special toy. You are trading with the kitten, not stealing his food or punishing him.

Growing kittens are voracious eaters, and any kitten that doesn't eat well should be checked by your veterinarian. Often the cause will be constipation and the remedy will be much the same as with a human baby—an enema or a mild laxative given as the vet prescribes. Never use a medication designed for dogs or humans on a cat without getting your veterinarian's approval first.

Foods to be avoided include chocolate in any form, especially for a small kitten (the massive amount of sugar that goes almost directly into the bloodstream can cause shock and even death), sweets, raw liver (often the cause of severe diarrhea), and milk. Yes, I know—kittens drink milk. However, with weaning comes a loss of the enzymes required to digest milk. The change is gradual and may require several months, but by the time they are six months to a year old most kittens no longer can digest milk, especially cow's milk. Overfeeding of milk even at three or four months may lead to severe diarrhea. Cheese, however, already is partially digested and causes few problems when presented in small amounts. In fact, many canned foods contain cheese.

Many kittens like rather unusual foods, especially various vegetables. We've had cats that loved baked and mashed potatoes, corn kernels, green beans, peas, and rice. In moderation all are good foods if the kitten likes them and has no problem digesting them. Pay attention to your kitten's litter box habits after giving any unusual foods. By the way, rice with ground beef mixed in often is an excellent remedy for diarrhea until the vet gives you something better. Some kittens develop a liking for potato chips, crackers, and other crunchy foods. Large amounts of salt are not good for a cat, but in moderation an occasional chip probably will do no harm although it certainly will do no good either.

I'm not sure what to suggest if your kitten develops a taste for pastas. A well-cooked noodle is harmless, but I wouldn't suggest regular meals of

Pet dental products are available for helping to fight plaque, reduce tartar build-up and control unpleasant breath. Photo courtesy of Four Paws.

spaghetti. Ketchup seems harmless, as does a bite of cheeseburger with all the fixings (except onions, which I think all cats must hate). As a general rule table scraps are not a good idea for kittens, but if a balanced diet of commercial prepared food is given every day they will do no harm. Avoid bones, both fish and chicken. Probably an adult cat's stomach can handle small bones, but it is best not to take a chance with a more delicate kitten. Beef bones rarely are attractive to kittens.

Cats usually ignore dog food, which is deficient in protein and fats. Apparently most cats think dog food also smells odd. Few cats will try to nibble on a hard dog biscuit, or any hard food for that matter. Chew bones and rawhide strips hold little attraction for a kitten other than something to bat around. Oddly enough, most dogs will eat almost anything a cat will eat and gulp it down with relish, but the high protein content of cat food may cause sores in the dog's mouth and certainly is not good for the dog's nutrition.

A healthy kitten should be full of activity and interested in its surroundings.

GROOMING

With the exception of the Sphynx and perhaps a couple of other relatively rare breeds, cats are very hairy animals. In fact, it sometimes seems as though a longhair were just an eight-pound the year the "natural" cat only sheds the occasional batch of dead hair.

Unfortunately for our furniture, our cats are no longer "natural" cats. Because of electric lights

American Shorthair grooming her youngster. Felines are noted for their fastidious grooming habits, to which they devote a considerable amount of time.

ball of hair waiting to spread itself out on the couch, bed, or carpet. In nature cats react to changing day lengths and shed about twice a year, once in spring to get rid of the old winter coat and once in fall to put in the new winter coat. Each shedding or molting period should last about three weeks. The rest of they have fairly constant day lengths all year, with the amount of sunlight entering from a window not greatly affecting the molting cycle. For this reason the house cat now sheds all year, a little bit all the time and heavier masses often during the traditional spring and fall shedding seasons.

Though both longhairs and shorthairs have the same number of hairs, the extra length of each hair of a longhair makes it seem as though longhairs shed more than shorthairs. Regular grooming is the only practical method of reducing the amount of shed hair covering all stationary objects in the home.

Cats constantly groom themselves by licking the fur, even moistening the forepaws with their tongues to help groom the face. They also chew at their claws to help remove loose claw sheaths to expose the sharp claw underneath; this helps explain the sheaths you can find lying loose anywhere around the house.

Licking the fur serves a number of functions in the cat, and a kitten instinctively knows all the proper procedures. Obviously, licking serves as a type of dry bath, removing dust and oil from the fur and dislodging loose hairs. It also stimulates various skin glands that produce secretions to help waterproof the fur and thus aid in keeping the cat's body snug and warm. Licking also separates hairs that may have become stuck together. A coat in which each hair is separate helps retain heat better than one that is matted.

Much as we do, cats produce vitamin D through the action of sunlight on the skin. In a cat, the important vitamin-producing chemicals are partially in the individual hairs, so a sunbathing cat lying in an open window actually is working at making up its vitamin D requirements for the day. Licking the hairs after a sunbath allows the cat to ingest much of the vitamin.

Lastly, licking is a typical cat behavior done out of boredom or just for something to do when not sleeping. It also serves as what is known as a displacement behavior. The classic example of this is a kitten that scratches furniture. He knows that if you are present and see him scratching the couch he will be scolded or worse. Yet his instincts tell him to scratch the couch both for simple enjoyment and to help shed claw sheaths. You walk into the room just as he stretches up to start clawing. The two bits of information—I must claw, I must not claw—contradict each other, so he starts grooming himself furiously. At least until you leave the room, when command one—I must claw— again takes precedent and he proceeds to rip into the couch.

Grooming helps cut down on dead hairs lying about the house and also prevents matting, which can be painful to your pet. It also helps prevent the cat from swallowing too much hair when licking itself, which cuts down on the number of hairballs that form in the gut. All cats get hairballs and they usually are nothing to worry about. The kitten simply regurgitates the ball (often along with the previous meal) and goes about his business, leaving you to clean up the mess. Cats in general are great vomiters, and some seem to take a great amount of pride in how often they can drag you out of bed at three in the morning to console them and clean up messes. Only if hairballs get out of control and actually obstruct the gut do you have any problems and need to see a veterinarian.

Many different grooming combs and brushes are available to do all types of specialized tasks in kitten grooming. Unless you are planning on showing your animal, however, you really need only a few items for routine grooming. First, you must have a claw clipper. Your cat can survive well without brushing or combing, but its claws must be clipped regularly. Two basic types for cats are available: scissors and guillotines. Guillotines have a fixed circular opening into which the claw slips, a cutting blade then being moved out from under

the handle to clip the claw. I hate this type of clipper and feel they should not be used on cats. Every one I have seen is too large to fit the claw of a cat and obviously is a modified dog claw clipper. Dog and cat claws are not at all similar, the dog claw being a heavy, fixed, quite thick claw that usually is very blunt. Cat claws are slender, often strongly arched, and flattened from side to side before ending in a very fine point. If a blade moves from the front of a cat claw to the back, the claw twists and this hurts the cat. Even the best mannered kitten hates having

You can choose from a wide array of fine grooming products formulated especially for cats. Photo courtesy Rolf C. Hagen.

its claws trimmed, so you want the least stress possible. The scissors trimmers are very short-bladed blunt scissors with overlappping beveled notches in each blade. The cat's foot is held in one hand and the thumb presses against the base of the claw, forcing it gently out of its sheath. The claw tip goes into the notch in the scissors and is snipped off with little or no twisting. Because the point of a cat's claw usually is extended well beyond the living pinkish area ("quick") of the claw, cat claws seldom bleed if trimmed carefully. If minor bleeding occurs it will stop in a few minutes or you can put a dab of astringent powder (available at your pet shop) on the cut tip.

Every cat book states that you should groom your cat every day or at very least three times a week. This is all very nice in theory, but unless you have a show cat or a longhair that is extremely docile, you'll never do it. After a few weeks or months of regular daily combing and brushing you will become very bored by the procedure and the kitten probably won't appreciate it either. Many cats literally hate being combed and brushed; next to having the claws trimmed, it is the worse normal occurrence in their life. I know that the books say to start early and train the kitten to accept grooming, but it just does not work

that way with many animals: they hate being combed the first time you do it and they hate it even worse the thousandth time you do it.

Thus the grooming session is seldom an idyllic one, with the kitten purring away in your lap while you gleefully and gently comb and brush. More often it consists of one person holding all four feet of the kitten while you try to dislodge a few dead hairs without being bitten. If your kitten loves being groomed, bully for you. But don't be surprised if he hates it.

For routine grooming, you should have a moderately fine steel comb and a fairly hard brush. The comb is used to separate hairs and remove some of the mats, while the brush smooths and polishes. You of course wouldn't use the steel comb on the ears or about the face, and you have to be careful on the belly and in the armpits where the hair is thin, the skin delicate, and kittens very grouchy. Every time you hurt a kitten while grooming it puts another tic on its list of reasons to resent grooming. Mats tend to be especially common under the throat, on the belly, at the base of the tail, and in the armpits—all the delicate areas. The more often you comb a kitten, especially a longhair, the less chance of mats forming. So put up with the

46

screaming and try to comb at least once a week. Doing the back is not difficult, as many kittens equate this with simple petting; it's the undersurfaces that need the special attention.

When mats do form, especially in the summer, you have a minor problem. They can be separated by careful and tedious working with the thumbs and forefingers pulling them apart. There also are special mat rippers available that allow you to simply tear up a mat into smaller and more easily handled tufts of tight fur. When a mat is large and obviously painful (it is very much like wearing clothes that are too tight—each time a leg moves the mat pulls on the skin and may actually tear the skin a bit) it can be cut away at the base with blunt, slightly curved scissors. Of course, if you have a show cat you would not remove any hair without consulting a groomer, but that really is another book. The curved scissors also are handy for trimming dirty hair from around the anus. All kittens and most cats occasionally have days when a bit of feces will stick to the fur and then be flattened out and embedded in the hair as the kitten scoots around and tries to remove it. Removing feces from a dirty rump is one of those jobs that make you want to keep tropical fish. But I guess it is all worth the effort when you get repaid by a bit

of purring and some leg rubbing.

If the kitten's fur ever becomes really tangled and dirty, you probably should go to a professional groomer, pay your money, and have your kitten hate a stranger rather than you. Few cats like getting a bath and I would suggest not bathing a kitten unless absolutely necessary. In fact, I can't think of many things I would like to do less than giving a cat a bath. Our two eighteen-year-olds probably have had one or two baths in their entire lives, and I don't believe they are any the worse for not having more baths. Remember, cats have long memories and they seldom forget who or what caused them stress. If you want a friendly cat around for

There are products available that make cat grooming and flea management easier. Photo courtesy of Interplex Labs.

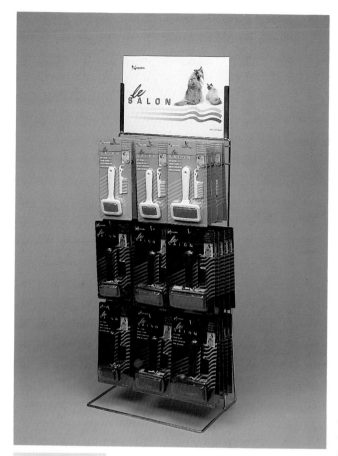

to spend a lot of his time trying to clean his ears. Even if no ear mites are present (a check for ear mites is part of the regular vetting procedure), excess scratching can lead to sores and infections at the base of the ear.

If the corners of the eyes become stained or slightly dirty, they can be cleaned with a cotton ball and some lukewarm water. Severe stains in white cats can be removed with special solutions available at your pet shop. Eyes that are perpetually dirty should be checked by a vet.

Also part of a regular vetting schedule is checking the teeth for looseness (with age) and tartar. I do not recommend that you try to brush your cat's teeth. Dry food helps keep the teeth clean enough in most cases. Many cats must be anesthetized to clean the teeth, and every time a cat goes under anesthesia there is a risk of serious side effects. Unless your vet recommends otherwise, don't worry about brushing teeth.

In summary, try to get your kitten to accept a complete combing and brushing at least once a week. Make sure that mats do not develop beyond control (small mats are easily felt during normal petting). Remove mats as soon as you find them. Trim the claws at least every two or three weeks, more often if necessary. Claw trimming is one grooming

Coat care is very important, especially for longhaired breeds of cat. Your pet shop dealer can help you choose the grooming tools most suitable for your cat. Photo Rolf C. Hagen Corp.

ten years or more, don't put any more stress on the kitten than you have to. Grooming is like a human haircut—you get one when you need it but you don't necessarily like to get one.

About once a month or so, you should gently wipe the inside of the ear with a cotton swab and a drop of mineral oil or (preferably) otic solution from your veterinarian. Excess wax serves as a good basis for an ear mite infection and also causes the kitten activity that must be done regularly and that can be done by an adult only. Keep an eye on your kitten's rear end for any dirty hairs or bits of stuck feces; any dirt should be removed as soon as seen or it will only get worse. About once a month clean out the ears

If they don't, put a dab of the jelly on a forepaw, from which they hopefully will lick it. If worse comes to worst, put an inch of jelly on your finger and stick it into the pouch at the corner of the kitten's mouth. Beware of teeth. It also is wise to give an inch or two

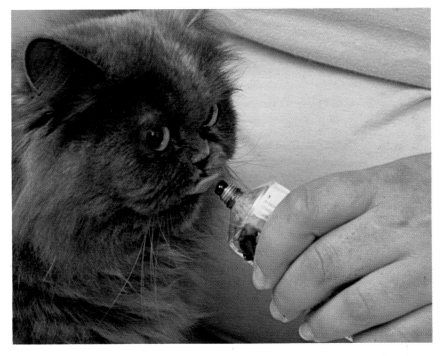

Administering a hairball remedy. Happily for your cat, many health remedies are formulated to be as pleasant tasting as possible. (Pictured: a blue Persian owned by Marianne Lawrence.)

with mineral oil or otic solution to remove excess wax and dirt and help prevent ear mite infestations. Clean the corners of the eyes as required.

One last grooming hint. About twice a month give the kitten an inch or two of flavored petroleum jelly with malt to help prevent hairballs. Most kittens enjoy the liver flavor and consider it a treat.

of jelly to the kitten each time he throws up a hairball or looks like he is gagging on a hairball. Several different brands of flavored petroleum jelly should be available in your pet shop, almost always as a tube very much like a tube of toothpaste. Some contain added vitamins and minerals, but the petroleum jelly and malt are what actually work on the hairball.

49

VETTING

Next to you, your veterinarian will be the most important human your cat will ever know. In today's world of rapid travel, diseases spread quickly and in ways that are not fully understood. A kitten that is perfectly healthy today can

kittens, will provide a full range of services including x-rays and blood tests, and will be convenient to where you live. His manner should inspire confidence just like a "people doctor." After all, a veterinarian also is a doctor and has gone through much the same

A marmalade kitten. Even if your kitty appears to be the picture of perfect feline health, it still needs regular veterinary care.

be very sick tomorrow, and only your veterinarian stands between serious illness and possible death. Do not be too casual about the health of your kitten. Although kittens are hardy little animals and cling to life very tenaciously, it really is a jungle out there.

When you start thinking of getting a kitten you should start looking for a veterinarian. A good vet will be interested in cats and

type of medical school training as your family doctor, including years of college study and an internship.

In much of the world, veterinarians are more or less divided between so-called large animal vets (basically horses, cattle, swine, sheep, etc.) and small animal vets (dogs and cats and, recently, birds). You will need a small-animal vet, not one interested in horses and cattle. Few veterinarians like to deal with both groups and may be uncomfortable working beyond their area of interest and expertise. Additionally, some veterinarians are not especially fond of working with cats, preferring dogs. Such a vet can be very curt with your kitten, which might not necessarily be bad, but it is poor bedside manners.

Your local telephone directory will provide you with a basic listing of local veterinarians. Try to talk to several and see how they feel about cats and if their practice can fit you in. There are many fewer vets than medical doctors in most areas but they have almost as many patients. Often friends or neighbors will volunteer information about their veterinarian. If they have had good experiences with their family vet, he or she is certainly worth a look.

Your kitten's first vet visit should occur within a day or two of when you get him. In some areas, consumer laws provide a period during which an owner must have the kitten vetted if various contract obligations (including guarantees and health refunds) are to work. Additionally, the sooner you get your kitten to the vet the more certain you will be that you have a healthy kitten. Be sure to make your appointment in advance.

During the first vet visit, your veterinarian will carefully check your kitten's general build and condition, take a look at the teeth, check for ear mites and treat them (most kittens have mites), and look for any signs of illness such as labored breathing or runny eyes or nose. Some vets routinely worm a kitten on the first visit because all kittens have worms. If he feels that something might be wrong, he might take a blood test and send it off for chemical analysis. He probably will want a stool sample, so collect some feces the night before and the morning of the visit and put it in a disposable covered container and refrigerate.

Your kitten's first vet visit will also mark his first vaccinations. Today it is standard procedure to give kittens shots for protection from feline distemper (panleukopenia) and the major respiratory diseases (viral rhinotracheitis and calicivirus) at between six and fourteen weeks. Although your kitten got some protection against these diseases from his mother's colostrum, this protection has now run out and must be initiated artificially.

In some areas the kitten's first rabies shot will be given as early as three months, but this varies greatly, depending on the local regulations and the vet's personal opinion. The first rabies shot can be painful and difficult for some

"Your kitten's first vet visit should occur within a day or two of when you get him."

kittens, so it seldom is given at a very early age.

Recently a vaccine against feline viral leukemia, a very serious disease, has become available. Some vets give the vaccination as early as nine weeks, some later, but your kitten should get the shot.

This will be only the first of several regular visits of your kitten to the veterinarian. The vet will want to check stool samples for worms again at about three months and probably at six months. By this time treatments should have eliminated the hoard of worms carried by kittens. I do not recommend the use of nonprescription wormers on kittens—wormers are poisons and kittens are delicate.

Also at about six months, the vet may want to give the first booster shots of the basic vaccinations. At that time you also will want to consult him about neutering the kitten, who will be starting to show signs of adult sexual behavior. Some veterinarians will spay a female as young as six months, while others prefer to wait another few weeks.

If you have a normal, healthy kitten that grows into a healthy cat, after the first year he will have to see the vet only once a year for a general check-up, annual rabies shot, and booster shots. Few cats are that healthy, however, and

little accidents can occur at any time that may require a veterinarian's attention. So stay in touch with your vet and keep his business card where it can be found readily. If there is an emergency veterinary hospital in your area, find out about it and keep a copy of their business card handy also. Even people often need treatment at odd hours and on holidays when the regular doctor is unavailable.

I guess I should mention cost, because someone has to pay for your vet's education, business overhead, and living expenses. Yes, vets do not work for free, but most are quite reasonable. Your kitten's examination and shots will probably cost less than half an equivalent human office visit. Rates vary widely from vet to vet and area to area, so if money is a problem, don't be embarrassed to ask about costs first. Many veterinarians offer time payments and may even take credit cards. Veterinary care is still a bargain compared to human medicine, and "human doctors" don't have to worry about being bitten and scratched.

VACCINATIONS

We just mentioned a few important vaccinations for your kitten, so I guess I should try to give you some information on the diseases being immunized against.

Vaccinations provide temporary protection against specific diseases in much the same way that colostrum protected the kitten for the first few weeks of life. Vaccines contain weakened or killed strains of disease organisms that have been specially produced to trigger the kitten's immune system. The immune system reacts to specific chemicals produced by disease organisms (antigens) to produce corresponding chemicals to combat the disease (antibodies). Antibodies are in the blood stream and lymphatic system and are constantly on the alert for the antigens. By promoting the production of antibodies, vaccinations give the animal protection against the disease. Because vaccinations only trigger the immune system for a certain period of time, booster shots are necessary at specific intervals to give the immune system an extra jolt.

Vaccines are produced under very exacting conditions and have been subjected to numerous tests of their safety. It is virtually unheard of for an immunization to actually cause the disease, although sometimes a shot can produce side effects such as pain and nausea for a day or so, much the same way that some humans react to tetanus shots, for instance.

Worms and other internal and external parasites do not respond

to vaccinations, so they must be treated directly with various chemicals that actually kill them or prevent them from reproducing. This is why vets are constantly battling against what could be called nuisance parasites such as roundworms, tapeworms, and fleas. So far no satisfactory vaccinations exist for these parasites, only for bacteria and viruses and similar microorganisms.

Feline distemper, more formally known as feline panleukopenia, is a deadly disease that is highly contagious, has a high mortality rate in kittens, and has almost no symptoms. A kitten may be perfectly healthy at breakfast and dying by midnight. Additionally, all the kitten's fluids, including urine and moisture from sneezing, may contain the virus and immediately spread it to any other cats in the vicinity. Humans can serve as carriers from one household to the next as well,

Some people think that because cats are so independent, their needs for care are minimal. This is not true: if a cat is to thrive, nutritional and veterinary needs must be met.

although we show no actual reaction to the disease. Even contaminated bedding or floors may be able to carry the disease to a cat just wandering by.

Obviously this is a disease that you do not want to fool with, so it is one of the first diseases for which the kitten is immunized. Distemper alone is an excellent reason to bring your kitten to the vet immediately after you get him.

You can think of the next two diseases as a type of cat flu. Both are upper respiratory illnesses brought on by different viruses and together causing over three-quarters of all serious respiratory illnesses ("colds") in cats. The first and most serious disease, feline viral rhinotracheitis, has a high mortality rate in kittens although older cats usually recover. It is marked by the usual sneezing, runny nose and eyes, fever, and lethargy that mark most "colds." It is highly contagious, and older cats can serve as carriers to kittens. Feline calicivirus disease is not as deadly as rhinotracheitis, but it is an extremely painful disease marked by ulcers on the tongue and palate. Obviously a kitten will not be able to eat, which further stresses him and may lead to even more serious complications such as pneumonia. This is another highly contagious disease, and it is very common in kittens.

Rabies is a disease whose very name strikes fear in people, with good reason. It is one of the few cat diseases that can be transmitted to humans and can be fatal to both. The U.S. Centers for Disease Control in 1987 recorded 166 verified cases of rabies in American cats, almost as many as in dogs (170). Of course rabies is still a rare disease in domestic animals (there were over 3,300 cases found in raccoons and over 2,000 in skunks), but it is one hundred percent fatal in infected cats. If your cat is allowed to roam, it has a good chance of coming into contact with a diseased raccoon or skunk, and once infected, it is as good as dead. Adding to the terror is that infected animals readily transmit the disease to humans through superficial bites or even scratches, the saliva carrying a multitude of the virus. Unless treatments are started in humans before symptoms appear, rabies is fatal in humans.

This dread disease attacks the brain and spinal column and its most obvious symptoms consist of drastic changes in personality, the cat either hiding (dumb form) or turning extremely vicious (furious form). Either way, death occurs in a few days and the animal is a definite menace to human life as well.

Because rabies vaccines once were fairly dangerous to the

"Rabies is a disease whose very name strikes fear in people, with good reason. It is one of the few cat diseases that can be transmitted to humans and can be fatal to both."

54

animal (cat rabies vaccines are very different from dog vaccines) and cat rabies was considered to be rare, many areas do not yet require that cats be vaccinated against rabies. Regardless of whether or not it is required by law, have your kitten vaccinated. Even if you plan on never letting him out of the house (a wise idea), keep up the series of annual or triennial boosters as well. In the case of rabies it is much better to be safe than sorry, or even possibly dead.

One last disease to consider is feline leukemia, actually a complex of viral diseases with varying symptoms. In just the last few years a simple blood test has been developed to detect this disease in older cats, and a vaccine now exists to prevent it in kittens. Because the symptoms are so variable, the actual disease is hard to detect other than by the blood test, but it can lead to serious debilitation and eventual death. If your vet offers the vaccination, take advantage of it so you will have one less disease to worry about.

Immunizations for other diseases are constantly being developed, and your veterinarian may be able to protect your kitten from other diseases. Follow his advice and respect his expertise. For instance, if a vaccine for Lyme disease, a recently noticed serious disease carried by ticks, were to become available soon (as may be the case) you would want your kitten protected. No one wants to see an animal suffering needlessly if a preventive shot is available.

NEUTERING

Although your kitten officially is not an adult until the age of a year, when growth stops, sexual maturity comes long before adulthood. A female kitten only five months old may have heat cycles and be able to be mated and give birth. A male matures a bit slower, but by eight or nine months he will start spraying and the other behaviors associated with a tom cat.

I believe that neutering, the process of making a

KENNEL CAB II

cat sterile, is one of the most important issues of cat care and must be considered by anyone who keeps a cat. Cats reproduce at a rate much higher than the number of available homes increases. There are always unwanted kittens that unthinking people either abandon or kill. If you let your unneutered cat roam, you will be directly responsible for kittens. Perhaps they will not be in your house, but they will be somewhere, a shed or gutter. Rule number one to prevent this is "never let your cat roam." Fact number one is "all cats escape at some time or other." Rule number two is "neuter your cat." Fact number two is "neutered cats do not produce kittens."

Please, for everyone's sake, unless you are breeding purebred show cats, have your kitten neutered.

Your veterinarian will give you the details of exactly when he thinks it is best to "fix" your kitten, but in general, females are spayed either at four to six months (before the first heat cycle) or at six to eight months (after the first heat). Different vets have reasons for preferring one time or another. Spaying a female is more complicated than fixing a tom, as it involves actual internal surgery under anesthesia. The kitten's ovaries and uterus are removed, making sure that not only will she

be unable to produce kittens, but she will no longer have heat cycle—ever. No more yowling, no more trying to escape all the time, no more odd smells.

Because surgery is involved, the female may have to stay with your vet for a day or two to recover from anesthesia. When she comes home she will be out of sorts for a couple of days and her appetite may be weak. Offer healthy treats and make sure she always has water. It is best to confine her in her carrier at first or at least keep her in a small room where she cannot be too active. She will appear to be constipated for two or three days, but this seldom is anything to worry about. Because she will have a series of stitches holding together the incision in the belly, handle her carefully especially when picking her up. If the stitches should rip you will see a bit of bleeding and you should call the vet for advice. After about ten to fifteen days the incision should be healed enough for the stitches to be removed, so you will be bringing her back to the veterinarian's office for a brief visit.

Toms have the testes in an external sac or scrotum located just below the anus. To be neutered he is given a heavy dose of tranquilizer, enough to make him unaware of what is happening but probably not fully comatose.

> "There are always unwanted kittens that unthinking people either abandon or kill. If you let your unneutered cat roam, you will be directly responsible for kittens."

The vet makes two small incisions in the scrotum, pops out both testes, and cuts the cords. Bleeding is minimal and stitches usually are not required. Antibiotic may be applied to the incision, but healing usually is quick and uncomplicated. I recently saw a tom being "fixed" on a kitchen table by a vet performing a house call. The whole operation was completed in fifteen minutes or less and the cat was back on his feet by the next day. Gradually the scrotum shrinks and disappears under the hair, leaving few visible signs.

Because a male kitten begins to spray at about nine months, sometimes earlier, you want to have him fixed before he develops this habit. For this reason many vets like to do neutering as early as seven months. Discuss this with your vet, before the spraying begins.

Fixing a tom is an inexpensive procedure since an overnight stay usually is not required and there is no real surgery. A female spaying may cost three or four times that of a male neutering. The operations must be performed, however, and many vets have discount schedules to promote spaying and neutering even of semi-wild farm cats or tame alley cats. Veterinarians realize the importance of slowing the growth of the unwanted kitten population and will do whatever they can to help you. Do not be afraid to discuss prices and any of your fears with your vet. Neutering does not make a cat fat and lazy, but it does make him or her friendlier (especially toms) and easier to keep in the house.

Please neuter your cat!!!

Cats love to play with objects that can be batted about and chased, and sharing the "game" with a pal is even more fun. Even better, these vigorous activities help to keep a cat well-exercised.

SUGGESTIONS

This chapter will discuss a bunch of miscellaneous topics that are important to kitten ownership and care but just didn't fit well into the previous chapters. (Also, I simply forgot to talk about one or two of these topics earlier and this

insecure for a few days until he gets used to the new house and people. The first day should be spent confined to one room complete with a litter box, the carrier with a cushion to serve as a bed, and food and water dishes.

is as good a place to mention them as elsewhere.) Let's go back to the beginning and see what happens when the kitten first goes home with you.

Remember that you are bringing home a small, delicate animal that is used to kittens and mother, not a bunch of humans. He will be very

Two or three toys should be available too, but he may not play much at first. If you have other cats or dogs, keep them away from the kitten for a couple of days and watch all interactions carefully. Dogs probably won't bother the kitten (dogs and cats are not natural enemies, at least in a house), but an older tom might be unhappy at the competition. Few animals will harm a kitten, and it is amazing what a kitten can sometimes get away with. Tippy spent a good part of her third and fourth months curled up sleeping on the tail of Punkin, a forty-pound Samoyed.

Never bring home a kitten just before a holiday party or other large gathering of people. They simply cannot tolerate the noise and activity of more than a few strangers at first. The same principle applies with children—children should handle young kittens only under supervision at first, and only one child at a time should play with the animal. Children must be taught that kittens are not toys, although they can be played with gently, and that they should expect kittens to occasionally bite or scratch to show they are being mistreated. Personally, I doubt that children under eight or nine years old should even have pets, but I realize that this is an extreme view.

Never give a kitten as a gift to someone who is not expecting to get one. They are not surprise gifts to put under a Christmas tree or in a stocking, regardless of what television and the movies tell you. Many cat breeders will not even sell kittens less than two or three weeks before Christmas just to prevent this. Now if only mall pet shops would adopt this practice as well there would be fewer kittens looking for homes by New Years.

Kittens are able to get into more trouble than you would ever believe, but usually they survive. It is part of your responsibilities as a cat owner to give them every chance at a long life. Your house must be "kittenproofed" as much as possible, and before the kitten is allowed to roam.

One of the deadliest items in a home is your basic electrical cord. Kittens are drawn to cords (perhaps they can sense the flow of electricity?) as iron filings to a magnet. Their needle-sharp teeth go right through the thin insulation of most cords, right into the metal. Assuming the electrical shock they receive is not serious (which may not be the case), they probably will get minor to major burns on the roof of the mouth. At the very least, expect a shocked kitten to be disoriented and lack an appetite. An emergency trip to the vet is essential. The obvious solution is to make sure unattended kittens cannot get at live electrical cords. Notice also that a kitten's chewing of insulation can lead to short circuits and even fires, so be very careful. You also want to cover unused outlets with plastic protectors, because little claws will search out any small hole to play in.

Make sure there are no holes in

the baseboards or lower walls into which a kitten could disappear. In their curiosity to follow unusual scents and check out every cave, a kitten can easily disappear into a hollow wall and wander about, wailing for hours, until you can coax him out.

Never leave water in a bathtub, sink, or large pan. Drowning is easy if you are only six inches high. Many kittens are attracted to running water, so accidental scaldings are something to be considered. Open toilet lids are an obvious danger both from drowning and from drinking the usually poisonous toilet bowl cleaners in the water.

Kittens like to follow people, which can lead to obvious accidents such as being stepped on, but also remember that kittens do not understand doors and can be easily crushed in a second. Screen windows and balconies to prevent accidental falls.

Kittens have a desire to taste things and play with anything lying about. This makes them very susceptible to poisoning from many common household chemicals, especially those likely to be found under the kitchen sink or in a workshop. They also can swallow pins and needles and staples.

Many household plants are poisonous, at least in theory. Common dangerous plants include such things as English ivy, dumb cane (dieffenbachia), poinsettia, anything in the lily and amaryllis families, and philodendron. It is unusual for kittens to actually eat enough of a poisonous plant to be affected, because the taste usually is bitter and many produce a stinging sensation as soon as they are chewed. Vomiting and an upset stomach are more normal consequences than serious illness.

Insect stings are always possible, as bees and wasps are everywhere. House centipedes, the very long-legged brown things that go running over the bathroom ceiling and seem to be all knees, can produce a mildly venomous bite if attacked.

I don't mean to make the average home sound like a house of horrors, but I guess reality makes it so from a kitten's viewpoint.

When I listed the items you should buy along with the kitten, I purposely did not mention leashes and collars. Frankly, I do not believe that cats are meant to walk on leashes, and any attempt to make them do so is a stupid stunt. However, many people do successfully train their kittens to leash, so it is not impossible. (But I still wonder why anyone would want to do this.) The basic trick is to use a figure-eight harness of leather or plastic and not a collar. Most kittens can manage to wriggle out of a collar or at least get stuck in it, either wedging the lower jaw under the collar or managing to get one or both front legs passed partially through. A figure-eight harness passes around both front legs, with the leash connected at midback. Some have extra retainer straps over the chest much like a horse harness. A typical walk with a kitten is a series of rolls and entanglements, followed by picking up the kitten and walking back home. You may get exercise but the kitten just gets annoyed.

Actually, I'm exaggerating, as even I have had a couple of cats that walked fairly well on a leash. I just sincerely don't understand what anyone—cat or owner—gains by this.

Speaking of collars, what about flea collars? If you live where the temperature rises above freezing for more than two or three months a year, you probably have fleas in your house and on your cat. In addition to causing the kitten annoyance (kittens seem to draw fleas like honey draws flies) and making it scratch constantly, fleas carry tapeworms and probably are the major source of infection. Because the larvae (young stages) of fleas live in the carpet and in kitten bedding, an infestation cannot be treated in one step.

Flea collars are plastic strips impregnated with various

chemicals that kill fleas as they pass under and near the collar. Some of the chemicals used are very toxic and can cause side effects in sensitive cats. It is probably best not to put a flea collar on a kitten under three or four months old and thus avoid possible problems. Dog flea collars should never be used on cats, especially kittens, because kittens constantly lick themselves and swallow a lot of chemical that a dog never ingests. Read flea collar labels carefully. Those with pyrethrin, a natural insecticide made from daisies, perhaps are safest.

How about flea powders and sprays? The same precautions apply. Some are very toxic to

61

kittens, and those with pyrethrin are probably safest. Never mix flea powders, flea sprays, and flea collars—the mixture of chemicals could be lethal to anything under a couple of hundred pounds in weight. As with wormers, perhaps it is best to ask your veterinarian before buying anything to control fleas. Stay away from any sprays containing the chemical DEET—a lot of evidence suggests they are deadly.

Sprays to kill adult and larval fleas in carpeting and bedding are relatively safer because they are not actually on the cat. Be sure to follow instructions exactly, including the timing of repeated treatments. The new ultrasonic collars and modules are of uncertain value—some people think they work, but laboratory tests seem to indicate otherwise. I've used both and think that the small plug-in modules may work but the collar-mounted devices probably are too weak and small to do any good. If you keep pet rodents (mice, hamsters, gerbils) you cannot use ultrasonic anti-flea devices because the vibrations drive them literally crazy.

If you have never tried to give a pill or liquid medicine to a kitten, you are in for a treat. Basically, they do not like the idea at all and will do everything they can to resist. Liquid medicines are relatively simple. Using a plastic dropper (never glass, which can be broken in the mouth), insert the tip into the pouch at the back of the jaw, then through the gap behind the canine tooth and the molars (if your kitten is old enough to have molars). Don't squirt it in, but let it drop gently onto the tongue.

Pills are harder. Sit on the floor and hold the kitten between your legs, head out. Use one hand to grasp the upper jaw on each side and apply just enough pressure that the kitten will open his mouth a bit. With the other hand, put the pill at the back of the tongue. Now hold the mouth closed and stroke the throat to make sure the kitten swallows. Half the time you will find the pill on the floor fifteen minutes later and have to start over, but eventually it works. A simpler method is to wrap the pill in a bit of cheese or liverwurst and just let the kitten eat it. If you try to put the pill in the plate of food, the cat will show extreme sensitivity to pill textures; he has the ability to eat half a can of food and leave the pill behind, untouched. Some people are good at giving pills, others awful at it. A fact of life, I guess.

My last topic is one of the most important in this book, next to neutering, so it is fitting that it comes last where it will be somewhat obvious. This is your responsibility to keep your cat indoors at all times and never let it

"Never mix flea powders, flea sprays, and flea collars—the mixture of chemicals could be lethal to anything under a couple of hundred pounds in weight."

roam. I know this goes against everything you have ever heard about cats needing their freedom and the independence of cats. First, cats are no longer wild animals. They are completely domesticated, all romance to the contrary. If left to their own devices, cats will indeed revert to a semi-wild state and become feral. Large numbers of feral cats exist in any city, often surviving but not really living well.

A cat allowed to roam, even just near your home, is asking for trouble. Just think of the problems it can run into: automobiles, animal wardens, pesticides, lawn fertilizers, irate gardeners with hoes, small boys with slingshots and B-B guns, other and larger cats, raccoons, skunks, bees, small boys with tin cans, bicycles, vicious dogs, vicious dog owners, cat haters, flooded drains, poisoned foods, rat baits—the list could go on for pages. Do you really want to subject your kitten to this so it can have an elusive taste of freedom? Remember also that an unfixed cat's sexual habits will assure that a female in heat visiting with one or more males will return home pregnant.

Although animal wardens commonly enforce laws against dogs roaming free, they seldom try to catch roaming cats. Some areas don't even have laws restricting loose cats, which I feel is a real shame. If the owner cannot assume the responsibility of keeping his cat inside, then he at least ought to be made to pay for the privilege of causing problems. Roaming cats are notorious for digging up flower gardens and waiting for birds at feeders, both activities that can lead to trouble with the neighbors and the law.

If you value your kitten and want to keep him around for a while, with the least possible problems, then have him or her neutered and don't let him or her out of the house unattended. You owe at least this much to an animal that will give you years of companionship and pleasure.

Persian kits. Which would you choose? With kittens as adorable as these, the choice would not be easy!

INDEX